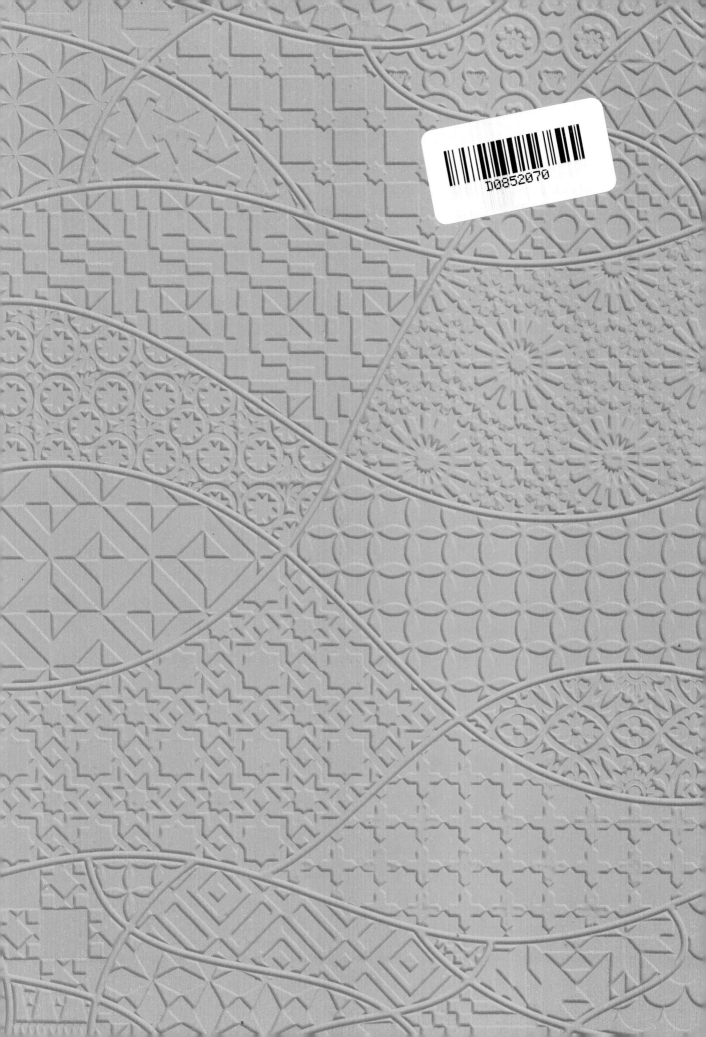

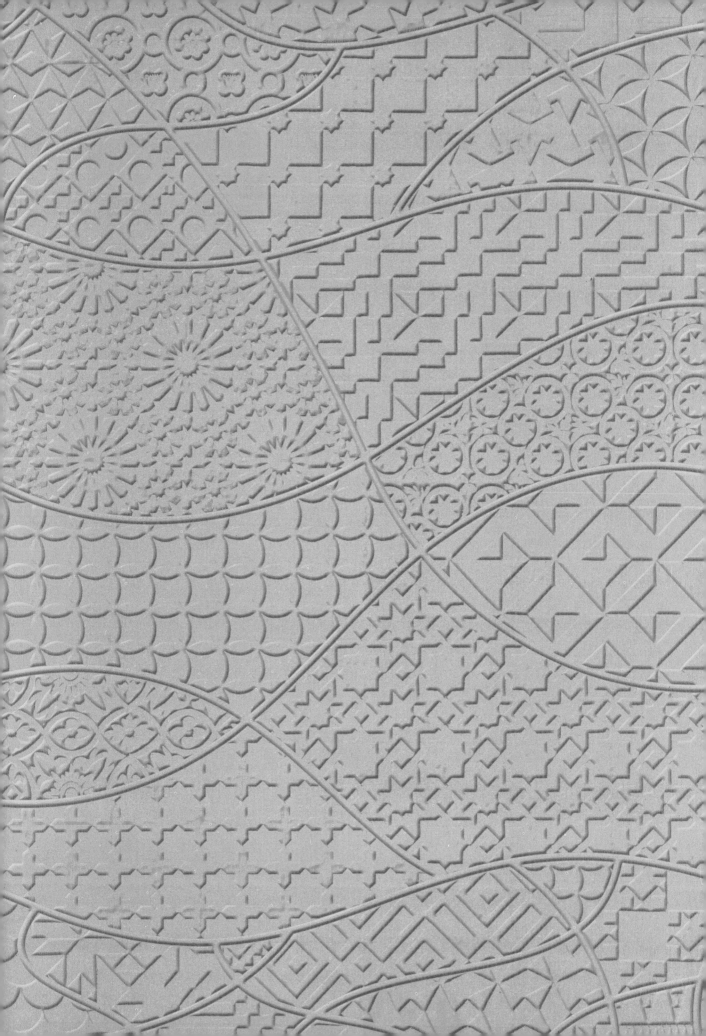

Avenues

Alfredo Schifini
Deborah J. Short
Josefina Villamil Tinajero

Erminda García
Eugene E. García
Else Hamayan
Lada Kratky

HAMPTON-BROWN

Grades 1–2 Curriculum Reviewers

Kimberly L. Barto
Teacher
Austin Parkway Elementary
Fort Bend Independent School District
Sugar Land, Texas

Cynthia Cantú
Bilingual Teacher
Eli Whitney Elementary
Pharr-San Juan-Alamo School District
Pharr, Texas

Barbara Ann Genovese-Fraracci
District Program Specialist
Instructional Services Center
Hacienda La Puente Unified
    School District
Hacienda Heights, California

Robin Herrera-Snitofsky
Language Arts Coordinator
Neff Elementary
Houston Independent School District
Houston, Texas

Lizabeth Lepovitz
Bilingual Teacher
James L. Carson Elementary
Northside Independent School District
San Antonio, Texas

Derek Lewis
ESOL Teacher
Bryant Woods Elementary
Howard County Public Schools
Columbia, Maryland

Susan Mayberger
Supervisor of ESL
Omaha Public Schools
Omaha, Nebraska

Dr. Mark R. O'Shea
Professor of Education
Institute for Field-Based Teacher
    Education
California State University,
    Monterey Bay
Monterey, California

Jessica C. Rodriguez
Bilingual Teacher
Manuel Jara Elementary
Fort Worth Independent
    School District
Fort Worth, Texas

Rita C. Seru
Bilingual Teacher
Thomas Gardner School
Boston Public Schools
Boston, Massachusetts

Liz Wolfe
Coordinator
Curriculum Services for
    English Learners
San Mateo County Office of
    Education
San Mateo, California

Ruth Woods
ESL Teacher
Lyndale Community School
Minneapolis Public Schools
Minneapolis, Minnesota

Acknowledgments

Every effort has been made to secure permission, but if any omissions have been made, please let us know. We gratefully acknowledge the following permissions:

Cover Design and Art Direction: Pronk&Associates.

Cover Illustration: Nadia Richie.

HarperCollins Publishers: *Mama Talks Too Much* copyright © 1988 by Marisabina Russo. Used by permission of HarperCollins Publishers.

Acknowledgments continue on page 203.

Hampton-Brown
P.O. Box 223220
Carmel, California 93922
800-333-3510
www.hampton-brown.com

Printed in the United States of America

ISBN 0-7362-1827-0

05 06 07 08 09 10 11 12 9 8 7 6 5 4

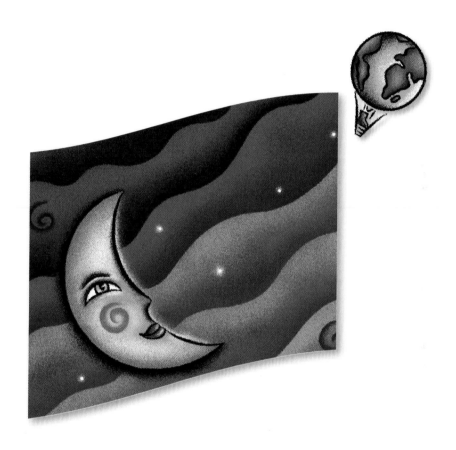

Avenues Go Everywhere

Everyone Needs a Home

Draw a Home

1. Draw a picture of a home.
2. Tell a friend what you like best about it.

Places We Live

apartments

house

mobile home

farmhouse

adobe house

cabin

Parts of a House

chimney····

roof

wall····

floor

window····

door

Welcome Home!

This is the **way** friends help each other.

Our friends **live** in the **house** next door. They need a porch. We **build** a porch together.

New Words

this

way

our

live

house

build

Read a Song

A **song** can tell a story with music and words.

✔ In this song, look for **words** that are used again and again.

Somalia

This is the way we build our house,

Nepal

build our house, build our house.

15

 Selection Reading

This Is the Way We Build Our House

by Susan Buntrock

Somalia

This is the way
we build our house,

Nepal

build our house,
build our house.

Guatemala

This is the way
we build our house,
with wood, stone, or leaves.

Ghana

This is the way
we paint our house,

Mexico

paint our house,
paint our house.

Argentina

This is the way
we paint our house,
the colors of the world.

This is the way
we dress up our house,

India

dress up our house,
dress up our house.

Japan

This is the way
we dress up our house
for happy holidays.

This is the way
we live in our house,

Florida, USA

live in our house,
live in our house.

Texas, USA

This is the way
we live in our
house, in the USA!

Think and Respond

Strategy: Main Idea and Details

What do the people in the song do?

This Is the Way We Build Our House

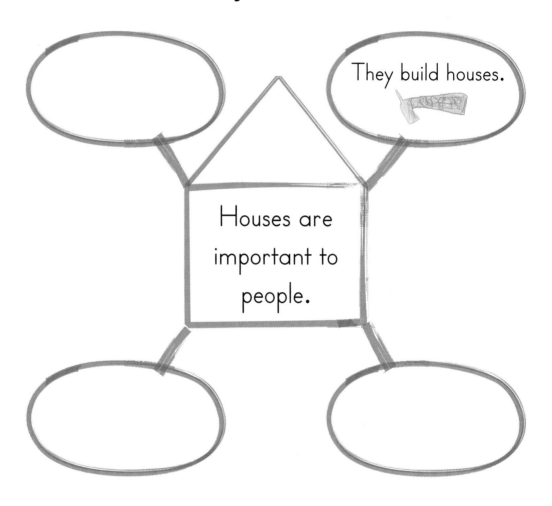

They build houses.

Houses are important to people.

Sing the Song

Sing the song together.

Act out the verses.

Use your map.

Talk It Over

1 Do you like the song?

Why or why not?

2 Name one thing you can do to a house.

3 How are the houses in the song different?

How are they the same?

The houses are made of different things.

Content Connections

Talk About Homes

partners

> My house is on land. This house is on the water.

1. Draw a picture of your home.

2. Draw a picture of a home in another place.

3. Talk about the pictures.

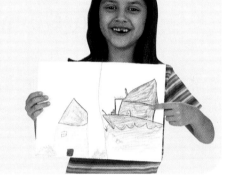

SOCIAL STUDIES

Learn About Countries
Internet

small group

1. Read the country labels in the story.

2. Find out facts about the countries.

3. Tell about the countries.

Argentina
People speak Spanish.

¡Hola!

Make a Safety Book

large group

1. Learn about how to be safe at home.

2. Make a safety book.

3. Share your safety book with your family.

My Safety Book

by Sara

Make a Dream House Poster

on your own

1. Draw a picture of your dream house.

2. Write about your dream house.
   Is it big or small?
   What is in it?

3. Share your dream house with the class.

My dream house is huge!

Make Predictions

When you guess what will happen next, you **make a prediction** .

 Look for clues.

? Guess what will happen next. = prediction

Listen to the story. Tell what will happen next.

The Three Pigs

The house is made of straw, so I think it will probably fall down.

Once there were three pigs. The first pig made his house of straw. One day a big wolf came by.

"Let me in!" said the wolf.

"No," said the pig.

"Then I'll blow your house down," said the wolf. He blew and blew.

Practice

Take this test. Make a **prediction**.

Listen to this part of the story and the question. Choose the best answer.

The wolf blew down the house of straw.
The second pig made his house of sticks.
The wolf came by.
"Let me in!" said the wolf.
"No," said the pig.

1 What will probably happen next?

○ The wolf will go away.
○ The wolf will blow the house down.
○ The house of sticks will stay up.

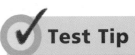 **Test Tip**

Think about all the choices. Then choose your answer.

 Song

Mouse House

Mouse had a **small** house,

   I was told,

Filled **with** **more** **than**

   It could hold.

Too many things

   Were on the floor,

So she swept them

   out the door!

Tune: "Here We Go!"

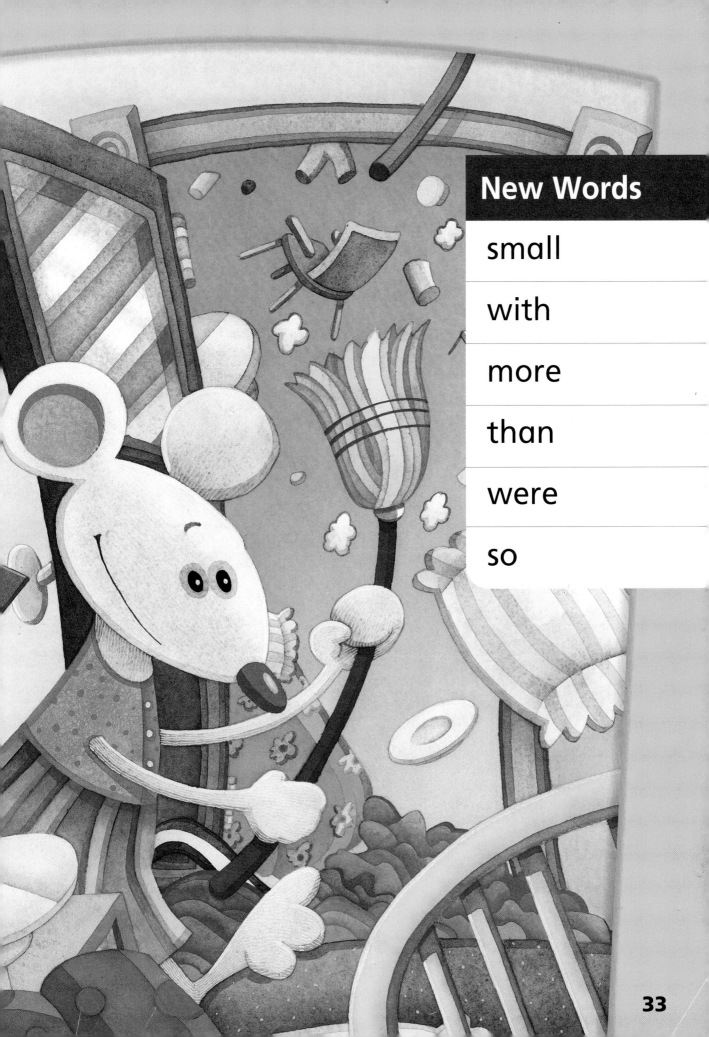

New Words

small

with

more

than

were

so

Honza's Little House

by Lada Josefa Kratky
illustrated by Alexi Natchev

Read a Play

A **play** is a story to act out.

"Honza's Little House" is a play.

Who is in the play?

Honza   **Mila**

Where does the play happen?

on a farm

Narrator

 Selection Reading

35

Once upon a time, there was a farmer named Honza. He lived with his family in a little white house.

Honza had a problem. So he went next door to see his neighbor Mila.

 Tell me, Mila, what can we do?
Our house is too small for us all!

 I will tell you what to do.
Ask the geese to live with you.

The geese moved in. There were geese on the table and geese on the chairs, geese on the dishes and geese on the stairs!

Honza went next door.

 Tell me, Mila, something more.
Our house is smaller than before!

 Then ask the hens to live with you.

41

So, the hens moved in.
There were hens in the window
and hens on the floor.

There were ten big hens.
Oh no, there were more!

 Honza went next door.

 Tell me, Mila, what to do.
Our house is small and messy, too!

Then ask the pigs to live with you.

So, the pigs moved in.

 There were pigs in the dresser, pigs on the bed, pigs on feet and pigs on heads!

The next morning,
Honza ran next door.

 Tell me, Mila, something soon.
We're completely OUT OF ROOM!

 Then send all the animals away!

49

And Honza did just that.

Out ran the geese,
and out ran the hens.
Out ran the pigs all the
way to their pens!

At last, all the animals were gone.

 Come in, Mila. Close the door!
Our house is bigger than before.

Honza smiles. Mila grins.
This tale is done. There is no more!

Meet the Illustrator

Alexi Natchev

When he was a child in Bulgaria, Alexi Natchev drew pictures of the folk tales he heard. Now he teaches people how to draw pictures for children's stories. Mr. Natchev says, "I like pictures better than words!"

Think and Respond

Strategy: Problem and Solution

Think about Honza's problem.

What happened first, next, and last?

What was Mila's solution?

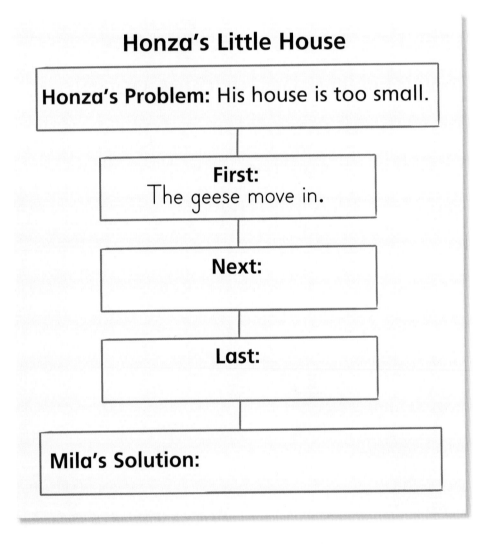

Honza's Little House

Honza's Problem: His house is too small.

First:
The geese move in.

Next:

Last:

Mila's Solution:

Retell the Story

Work with a partner.

Retell the play with a new ending.

Talk It Over

1 Would you like to live in Honza's house?

Why or why not?

2 What problem does Honza have?

3 Tell another story about a house.

How is it like "Honza's Little House"?

How is it different?

Content Connections

Direct a Drawing

partners

1. Draw a picture of a house.

2. Tell a friend how to draw the same house.

3. Talk about your drawings.

2+2   MATH

Count the Animals

small group

1. Make a shoebox house like Honza's.

2. Put some animals in the house.

3. Tell how many animals are in the house.

Show-and-Tell Clothing

Internet

1. Find out about clothing in another country.

2. Show the clothing. Tell about it.

These are <u>gomu</u> shoes from Korea.

partners

WRITING

Write a Thank-You Letter

1. Write a thank-you letter from Honza to Mila.

2. Share your letter with the class.

partners

Dear Mila,

I think my house is bigger than before. Thank you!

Your friend,
Honza

Questions and Answers

Listen and sing.

Song

Cake

Mama, Mama,
What will you bake?
Soon, my children,
I will bake a cake.

Mama, Mama,
When can we eat?
Soon, my children,
You will have a treat.

Tune: "Baa, Baa, Black Sheep"

Let's Learn!

A **question** is an asking sentence.
An **answer** is a telling sentence.

Question	Answer
1. **What is your name?**	My name is Yoko.
2. **Where do you live?**	I live on Oak Road.

Let's Talk!

Ask and tell about a favorite color.

What is your favorite color?

I like green.

Let's Write!

Write a question for a partner.

Ask the question.

Then write an answer to your partner's question.

Who is your friend?

Lisa

Show What You Know

Talk About Things We Need

Look back at the stories in this unit.

Make a web of things we need.

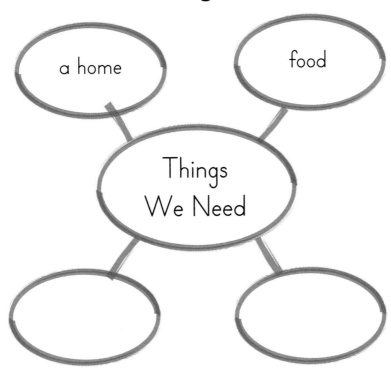

a home

food

Things We Need

Share Your Work

Draw a home.

Tell what you need in a home.

Read and Learn More

Leveled Books

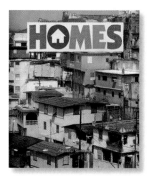

Homes
by Salvador Sarmiento

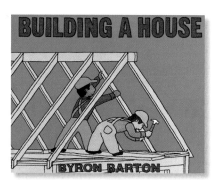

Building a House
by Byron Barton

Theme Library

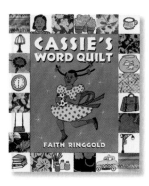

**Cassie's
Word Quilt**
by Faith Ringgold

Buzz
by Janet S. Wong

Internet
Go to: www.hbavenues.com
Build a House
House Hunt
At Home

Wings and Things

Make a Butterfly

1. Trace a butterfly pattern.
2. Cut it out.
   Paint it.
3. Talk about
   your butterfly.

Science Words

Growing Things

Some animals are **born** live.

cow   calf

Some animals **hatch** from eggs.

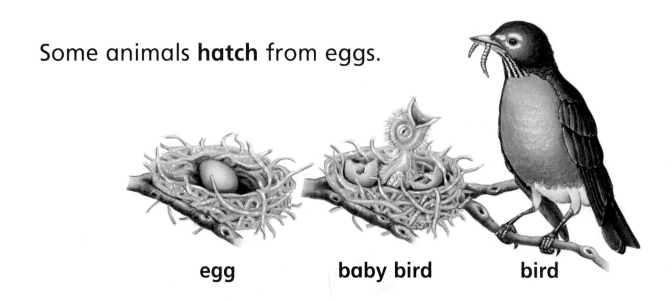

egg   baby bird   bird

Most insects **hatch** from eggs.

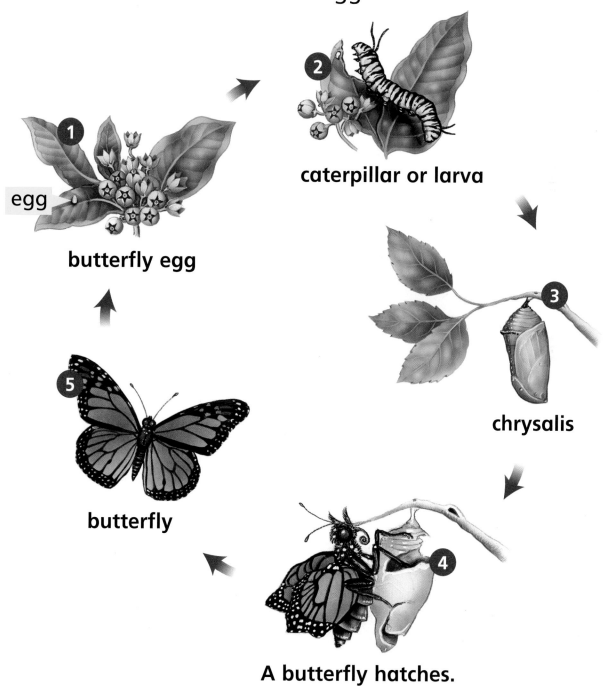

egg

butterfly egg

caterpillar or larva

chrysalis

butterfly

A butterfly hatches.

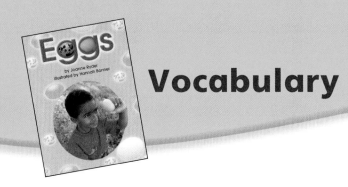
How Do You Make a Nest?

Act out the story.

1.

How do you **make** a nest?

First, I find some tall plants. Then I make a nest.

2.

How do you make a nest?

First, I find some dirt. Then I dig a hole. The hole is my nest.

3.

How do you make a nest?

I don't make a nest. I find some **water**. Then I lay **as** many eggs as I can!

New Words

how

make

first

water

as

Read a Science Article

A **science article** is nonfiction. This article tells facts about animals.

✔ Look for **headings**.
They tell you what each part of the article is about.

✔ Look for **captions**.
They tell you more about a picture.

 •••**Turtles**

This is a box turtle. A box turtle makes a nest for her eggs.

▼A box turtle lives on land, not in the water.••• caption

 Selection Reading

Eggs

by Joanne Ryder
illustrated by Hannah Bonner

Look at all the eggs! Many animals start life in an egg. There is food in the egg. The shell keeps animals safe.

All these animals hatch from eggs.

Animals and Their Eggs

Animal	Eggs
turtle	turtle eggs
frog	frog eggs
duck	duck eggs

Turtles

This is a box turtle. A box turtle makes a nest for her eggs.

▼ A box turtle lives on land, not in the water.

A Box Turtle Nest

A box turtle makes her nest at night.

1. First , she digs
   a hole with
   her back legs.

2. Next, she lays
   her eggs.

3. Last, she hides
   them with dirt.

In about three months, young box turtles hatch. They dig out of the nest. The tiny turtles are called hatchlings.

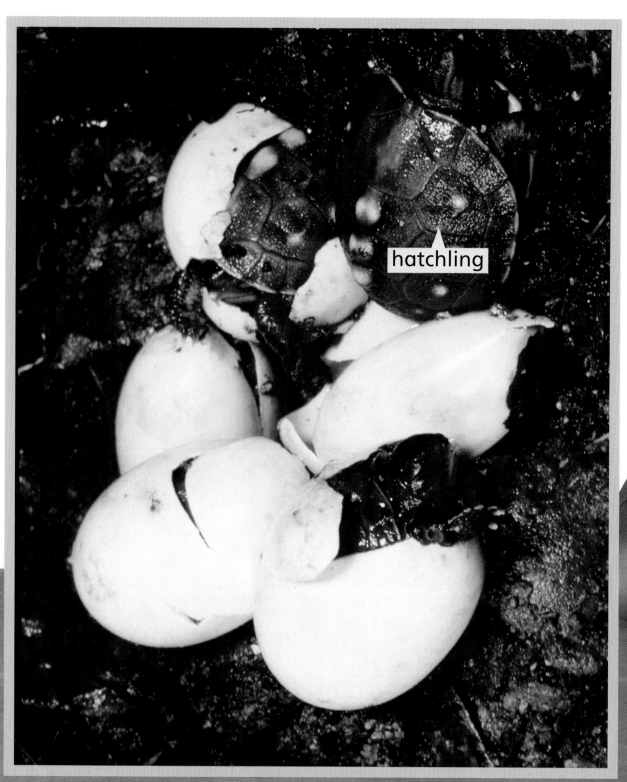

hatchling

Hatchlings are about as big as a nickel. Box turtles can live for many years. Some live for more than 100 years!

Frogs

This is a leopard frog. A leopard frog lays her eggs in the water.

frog eggs

How Frogs Hatch and Grow

In the spring, a frog lays thousands of eggs in the water.

1. First, little tadpoles hatch from the eggs.

tadpole

2. Then they begin to change into frogs. They grow legs. Their tails get smaller.

tail

leg

3. Last, the tadpoles change into small frogs by the summer. They eat and grow bigger. Look how they jump!

Ducks

This is a mallard duck. A mallard duck hides her nest in tall plants.

▼ A mallard duck can lay as many as 14 eggs.

How Ducks Make a Nest

Ducks make their nests with twigs, grass, and their own feathers.

1. The mother duck lays an egg every day or two for about ten days.

twigs

2. She sits on her eggs to warm them.

3. In about one month, the eggs hatch.

duckling

Now the mother duck leads her ducklings
to the water. They swim and eat and rest.

She quacks at her ducklings to keep them close. They will stay with her until they are grown. Then they will go out into the big world!

QUACK! QUACK!

Think and Respond

Strategy: Sequence

How do eggs hatch?

Choose an animal from "Eggs."

Tell what happens.

How Turtle Eggs Hatch		
First, the mother digs a hole.	Next,	Last,

Share and Compare Facts

Tell how different kinds of eggs hatch.

Use **first**, **next**, and **last**.

What is the same?

What is different?

Talk It Over

1 What animal in the story do you like best? Tell why.

2 What animal from the story can live for more than 100 years?

3 Think about the butterflies in *Waiting for Wings* and the animals in "Eggs."

What do these stories tell you about eggs?

Waiting for Wings and "Eggs" tell how some living things come from eggs.

Content Connections

Play a Life Cycle Game

small group

1. Look at "Eggs" again. See how the animals hatch and grow.

2. Act out hatching and growing for one animal.

3. Have friends guess the animal.

MATH

Talk About Egg Sizes

The goose egg is bigger than the snake egg.

partners

1. Make some egg cards.

2. Put them in order from smallest to biggest.

3. Make sentences about the eggs.

Make a Graph

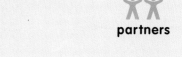
partners

1. Grow bean sprouts.

2. Measure the sprouts each day for three days.

3. Make a graph that shows how much your biggest sprout grew.

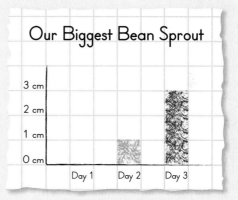

Our Biggest Bean Sprout

3 cm
2 cm
1 cm
0 cm

Day 1   Day 2   Day 3

WRITING

Write a Life Story
Internet

on your own

1. Pretend you are an animal.

2. Write about your life.

3. Draw pictures.

4. Read your story to the class.

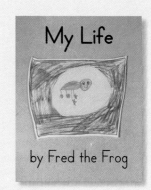

My Life

by Fred the Frog

Draw Conclusions

Use details in the story and what you already know to **draw a conclusion** .

details + (what you know) = A conclusion

Listen and find out about the mother bird. Why does she pretend to be hurt?

Mother Bird

The mother bird hears a fox! The fox could take her baby. She pretends that she is hurt. She drags one wing on the ground. The fox follows her away from the nest. Then the mother bird flies back to her baby.

It says the fox could take her baby. I know mother birds take care of their babies. I think she wants to save her baby.

Practice

Take this test. Draw a **conclusion** .

Listen to the article and the question. Choose the best answer.

How Animals Hide

Animals can use their colors to hide from other animals. A baby deer has spots on its coat.  The spots help the baby deer hide in the leaves. The arctic fox has brown fur. Its fur turns white in the winter.

1. Why does white fur hide the arctic fox?

○ Animals do not see the fox in the white snow.

○ White fur keeps the fox warm.

○ White fur makes the fox look like a baby deer.

 **Test Tip**

Think of your own answer. Then see if it is a choice.

Vocabulary

Song

Come Along!

I like to stay

Close to my home

When I play, but today

I did **something** new.

I **called** to some birds

Who were flying away,

And they **said** I could

Come along, too!

Tune: "Hey Diddle Diddle"

88

New Words

close

something

called

said

come along

89

Come Along, Daisy!

by Jane Simmons

Read a Story

This story is **make-believe** .

The animals act like people.

Who is in the story?

Daisy

Mama Duck

Where does the story happen?

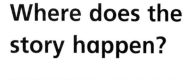

riverbank

reeds

on a river

 Selection Reading

"You must stay close, Daisy,"
said Mama Duck.
"I'll try," said Daisy.

But Daisy didn't.
"Come along, Daisy!"
called Mama Duck.

But Daisy was watching the fish.

"Come along, Daisy!"
shouted Mama Duck again.
But Daisy was far away,
chasing dragonflies.

"Come here, Daisy!" shouted
Mama Duck.
But Daisy was bouncing on
the lily pads.
Bouncy, bouncy, bouncy.
Bong, bong!

Plop! went a frog.
"Quack," said Daisy.
"Ribbit," said the frog.

Bong, plop!

Bong, plop!

Bong, plop!

Splash!

"Quack!" said Daisy,
but the frog had gone.
"Mama," called Daisy,
but Mama Duck had gone.
Daisy was all alone.

Something big stirred underneath her. Daisy shivered.

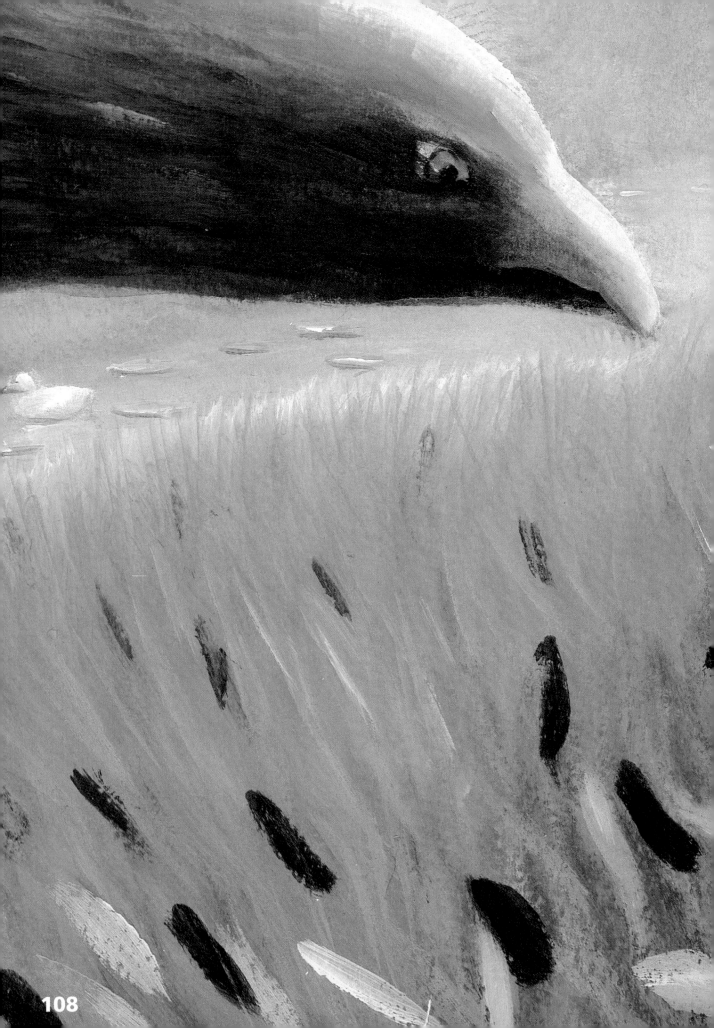

She scrambled up onto the riverbank.
Then something screeched in the
sky above!

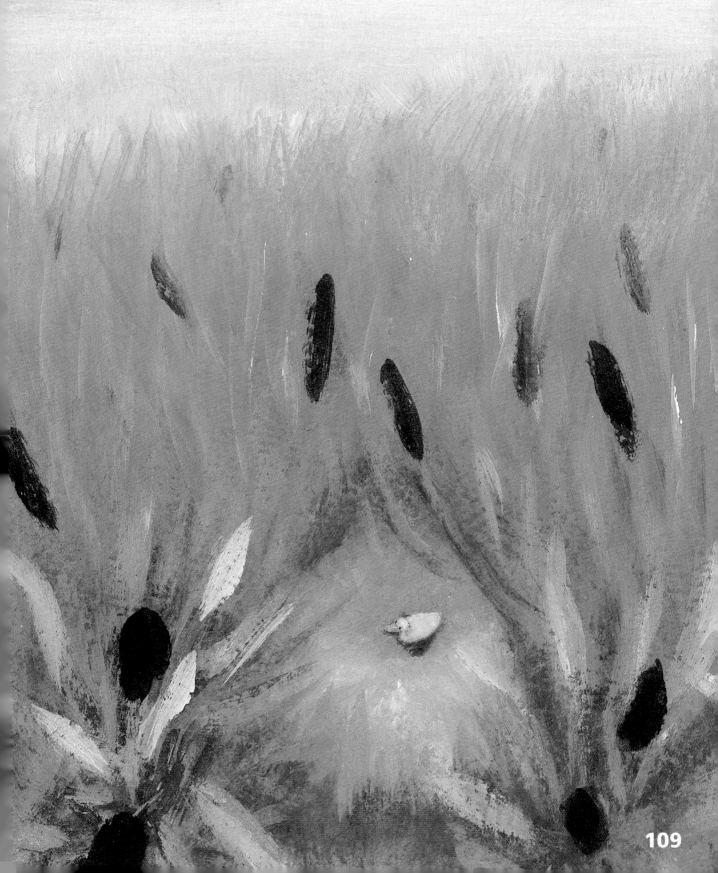

So Daisy hid in the reeds.
If only Mama Duck were here!

Something was
rustling along
the riverbank.
Daisy could hear
it getting closer . . .

. . . and closer,
and closer,
and
CLOSER . . .

It was Mama!
"Daisy, come along!" she said.
And Daisy did.

And even though Daisy played
with the butterflies,

she stayed very close to Mama Duck.

Meet the Author and Illustrator

Jane Simmons

AWARD WINNER

Jane Simmons loves to paint and write stories about Daisy the duck. She has written 14 of them! Ms. Simmons lives on a boat with a dog named Daisy, another dog named Pip, two birds, and a cat. From her boat, she watches many ducks swim and play, just like Daisy.

Think and Respond

Strategy: Story Events

What happens in the beginning, in the middle, and at the end of the story?

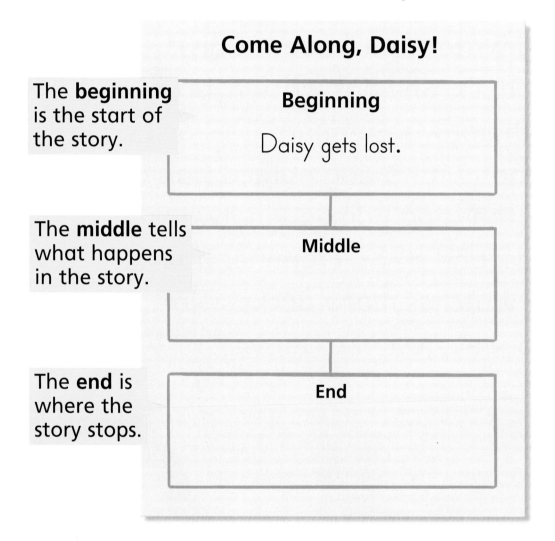

Come Along, Daisy!

The **beginning** is the start of the story.

Beginning

Daisy gets lost.

The **middle** tells what happens in the story.

Middle

The **end** is where the story stops.

End

Talk About Daisy's Feelings

How did Daisy feel when she was lost? Tell how she felt after Mama Duck found her.

Talk It Over

1 Which part of the story do you like best? Why?

2 Name one animal Daisy sees.

3 Look at "Eggs" and "Come Along, Daisy!" Which story could really happen? Which story is make-believe?

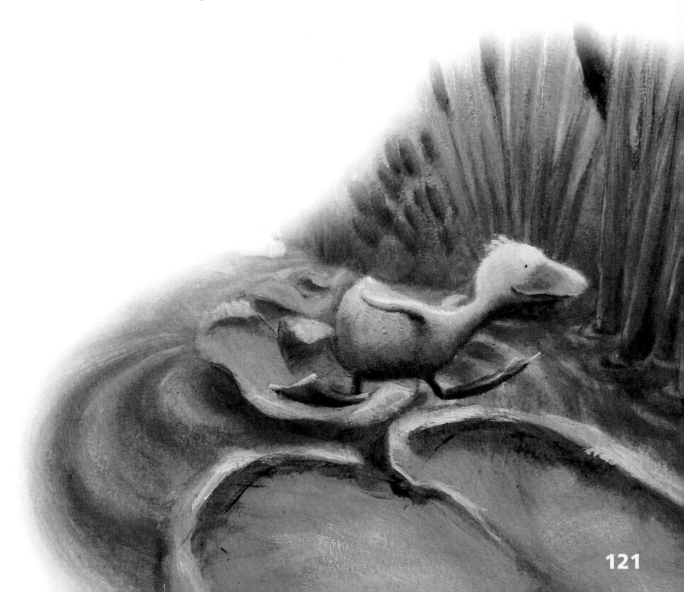

Content Connections

Make a Dragonfly Puppet

partners

1. Color and cut out a dragonfly puppet.

Daisy, I'll help you!

2. Pretend you are the dragonfly in the story.

3. Tell how you help Daisy.

MUSIC

Make Up a Song

Internet

large group

1. Write a song for Daisy.

2. Find music for your song.

3. Read "Come Along, Daisy!" and sing your song.

Draw a Habitat Mural

large group

1. Read about a habitat.

2. Draw a picture of the animals and plants that live there.

3. Tell about the habitat.

WRITING

Write a Letter to Daisy

on your own

1. Write a letter to Daisy while she is lost.

2. Tell her what to do.

3. Read your letter to the class.

> Dear Daisy,
>
> Please go home! Your mother misses you.
>
> Love,
> Lupe

Verbs in the Past

Listen and sing.

Song

Five Little Eggs

Five little eggs in the nest,
They rested in the nest.
Then one egg cracked,
And soon it hatched!
Four little eggs in the nest.

Tune: "Hickory, Dickory, Dock"

Let's Learn!

Some **verbs** end in **-ed**. They tell about an action that happened in the past.

Now	In the Past
1. The eggs hatch.	The eggs hatch**ed**.
2. The frog waits.	The frog wait**ed**.

Let's Talk!

Tell a friend about something you did yesterday.

I played with Sam.

Let's Write!

Write a sentence about what your friend did.

Draw a picture.

Share it with the class.

Anu watched a video.

Show What You Know

Pick Your Favorite Story

Look back at the stories in this unit.

Make a class chart.

Vote for your favorite story.

Stories We Like

Waiting for Wings	Eggs	Come Along, Daisy!
Simon	Ju	Elena
		Paul

Share Your Work

Draw your favorite animal from this unit.

Tell how it grows.

Read and Learn More

Leveled Books

Hello, Duck!
by Lada Kratky

Which Egg Is Mine?
by Sheron Long

Theme Library

Are You a Ladybug?
by Judy Allen and Tudor Humphries

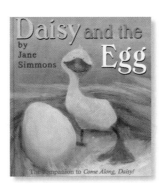

Daisy and the Egg
by Jane Simmons

Internet
Go to: www.hbavenues.com

Egg to Butterfly

Fun with Eggs

Who Lays Eggs?

Hello, World!

Share an Envelope

1. Draw a picture of yourself. Put the picture in an envelope.

2. Give your envelope to a friend.

3. Have a friend tell something about you.

Neha

Community Places

supermarket

post office

school

hospital

Goods

food

clothing

Services

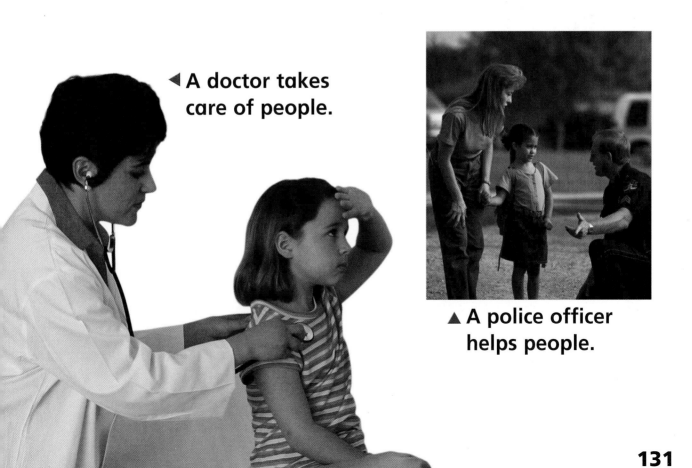

◀ A doctor takes care of people.

▲ A police officer helps people.

Nick's Day

Nick likes to **stop** and **talk** to all the people in his neighborhood.

Flower Shop

I **say** hello to Mrs. Goodwill.

I always **see** Mr. Lee go **by** my house.

Hi, Mr. Martínez!

Oh no! I talked **too** much. **Now** I'm late. Bye!

New Words

stop

talk

say

see

by

too

now

133

Mama Talks Too Much

by Marisabina Russo

Read a Story

Some stories are about things that could really happen. These stories are called **realistic fiction** .

Who is in the story?

Mama

Celeste

their neighbors

Where does the story happen?

in a neighborhood of a city

 Selection Reading

135

On Saturday mornings my mama and I walk to the supermarket.

I pull the folded metal carriage and run ahead as fast as I can. The wheels of the carriage go bump, bump, BUMP as they roll across the cracks in the sidewalk.

I run until I hear Mama calling, "Slow down, Celeste! Wait for me!"

Mama walks too slowly. But I wait while she catches up. At the corner she takes my hand, even though I think I'm big enough to cross the street by myself.

Then we see Mrs. Green and I say, "Oh, no!"

Mama stops. Mrs. Green stops. Now I have to stop.

"How are you?" says Mrs. Green.

"I haven't seen you in ages!" Mama says. "What's new?"

They talk and talk and talk.

Blah, blah, blah.

I watch the cars go by.
I count the red ones.
I count the white ones.

And then I tug at Mama's arm.
"Let's go," I say.

"Nice seeing you," says Mama.
"Call me!" says Mrs. Green.
At last we're on our way again.
Past the shoe repair,
past the Laundromat,
past the drugstore.

Then we see Mrs. Walker and I say, "Oh, no!"

Mama stops. Mrs. Walker stops. Now I have to stop.

"I've been meaning to call you!" Mama says.

"I've been sick all week," says Mrs. Walker.

"I'm so sorry to hear that," says Mama.

They talk and talk and talk. *Blah, blah, blah.*

I count the rings on Mrs. Walker's fingers.
I count the chains around her neck.
I count the bracelets around her wrist.

And then I tug at Mama's pocketbook.
"Come on, Mama," I say.

"I'll call you," says Mama.

"Don't forget!" says Mrs. Walker.

At last we're on our way again.

Past the fruit stand,

past the bakery,

past the newsstand.

Then we see Mr. Chan and I say, "Oh, no!"

Mama stops. Mr. Chan stops. Now I have to stop.

"I didn't see you at the tenants' meeting," Mama says.

"What did I miss?" asks Mr. Chan.

"They talked about cleaning up the basement," says Mama.

They talk and talk and talk.

Blah, blah, blah.

I watch the traffic light turn from green to yellow to red. I count the seconds between each color. I watch the light turn from red back to green.

And then I tug at Mama's jacket.

"Can we go now?" I say.

"Hope to see you at the next meeting," says Mama.

"I'll be there," says Mr. Chan.

At last we're on our way again.

"Mama," I say, "you talk too much!"

"Celeste," says Mama, "you walk too fast!"

"You stop too much to talk and talk and talk," I say.

"Look!" says Mama.

I say, "Oh, no!" It's Mrs. Castro.

Here we go.

Blah, blah, blah.

Then I see Mrs. Castro is holding a long red leash with a puppy at the other end.

"Can I stop to pet it?" I ask.

"I thought you were in a hurry!" says Mama.

But we stop, and I kneel down.
The puppy licks my cheek. Mrs. Castro
tells me his name is Jake. He's only ten
weeks old, and she just bought him some
toys. She shows me the squeaky rubber
fire hydrant and the yellow rubber ball.

"Isn't he cute?" I say to Mama.

Mama is laughing. "Talk, talk, talk," she says.

"Come visit Jake later," says Mrs. Castro. "I have to get going."

"We have to go, too," says Mama.

Then Mama and I are on our way
again. I slow down so I can walk
with Mama. We talk all the way to the
supermarket. We talk and talk and talk.

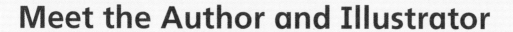

Meet the Author and Illustrator

Marisabina Russo

AWARD WINNER

When **Marisabina Russo** was a girl in New York City, a neighbor taught her how to draw. She started writing stories, too. Now Ms. Russo has a special place in her house to draw, paint, and write stories. She says, "Painting the pictures is the most fun of all."

¡Hola, niño!

"¡Hola, niño!"
Mr. Santos greets me
when he meets me
in the street.

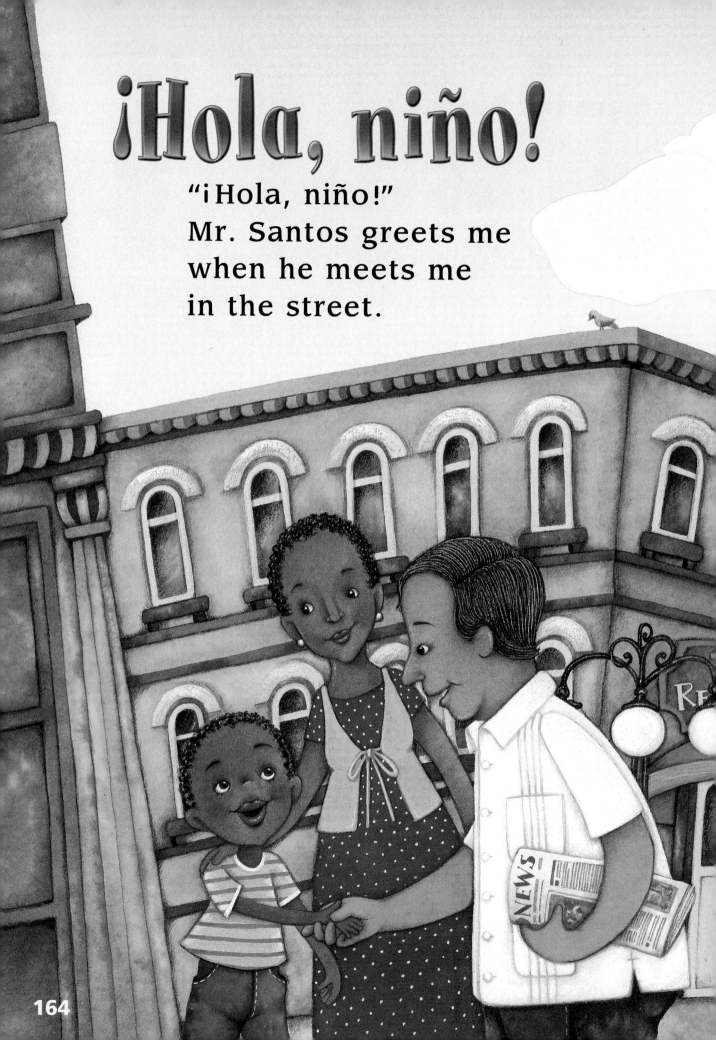

I never knew
what to say
before.

Now when he calls
"¡Hola, niño!"
I say "¡Hola, señor!"

—Lilian Moore

165

Think and Respond

Strategy: Characters

To learn about a character, you can:

✔ look at what the character does

✔ think about what the action means.

Mama Talks Too Much

Character	What the Character Does	What This Shows About the Character
Mama	stops to talk to everyone	She is friendly.
Celeste		

Act Out a Scene

Pretend you are Celeste or Mama.

Use what you know about them to act out a scene with a group.

Talk It Over

1 Talk about the neighborhood in the story. How is it like your neighborhood?

2 Where are Celeste and her mother going?

3 Think about the setting in this story.

Think about the settings in other stories you have read.

Tell about the different settings.

Some people live in the country. Some people live in the city.

Content Connections

Greet Your Neighbor

partners

1. Tell a partner about your neighbors.

2. Act out how to greet your neighbors.

3. Tell them how you feel about them.

I'm so happy to see you!

SCIENCE

Make a Safety Poster

small group

1. Walk around your school and neighborhood.

2. Draw the signs you see.

3. Make a safety poster.

4. Tell why signs keep us safe.

Be Safe! Read the Signs!

Make a Chart

My favorite store is the toy store!

large group

1. Make a chart of the stores in your neighborhood.

2. Tell what you can buy. Tell who works there.

3. Vote for your favorite store.

WRITING

Write a Newsletter

Internet

small group

1. Write about your town or city.

2. Put the news in a newsletter.

3. Share your newsletter with others.

Glenwood News

Kids Help Out

Last Friday, Mr. Moreno's class helped clean up Taylor Street. (See page 2 for more.)

Who's New?

Find out on page 3.

Make Inferences

Sometimes a writer does not tell you everything in a story. When you figure out something on your own, you **make an inference**.

what the writer says + what you know = Inference

Listen to the story. How do the characters feel?

A Trip to the Library

One day Sunil and Samir want to go to the library on Elm Street. They walk to Elm Street.

"Oh, no!" says Samir. He looks around. "Where is the library?"

"I think we're lost!" says Sunil.

"I do, too!" says Samir.

In the story the boys think they are lost. I'm scared when I'm lost. I think the boys are scared, too.

170

Practice

Take this test and make an **inference** .

**Listen to more of the story
and the question.
Choose the best answer.**

Sunil and Samir keep walking on Elm
Street. Then Sunil sees a blue sign.
"Here is the library!" says Sunil.
"I'm glad we found it!" says Samir.

1 How do the boys find the library?

   ○ They ask for help.
   ○ They use a map.
   ○ They read a sign.

 **Test Tip**

When you see
the word **How**
in a question,
look for an
answer that
tells how.

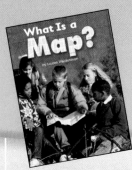

Song

Our Map

My daddy and I

Always **use** a **map**.

It **shows** each **place** we go.

We meet new **people**,

And we see new **things**,

And then come safely home.

Tune: "I Love the Sun"

New Words

use

map

shows

place

people

things

173

Read a Social Studies Article

A **social studies article** tells about the things people do. This article tells how people use maps.

✔ Look for **maps**.
A map shows what something looks like. A diagram is a type of map.

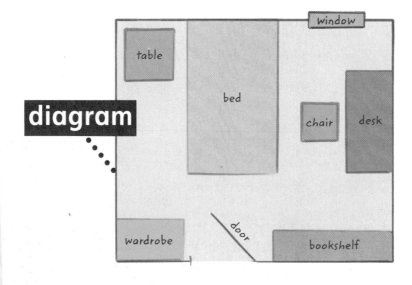

What Is a Map?

by Lauren Weidenman

What Is a Map?

A map is a drawing that shows what a place looks like from above. This picture shows what a beach looks like from above.

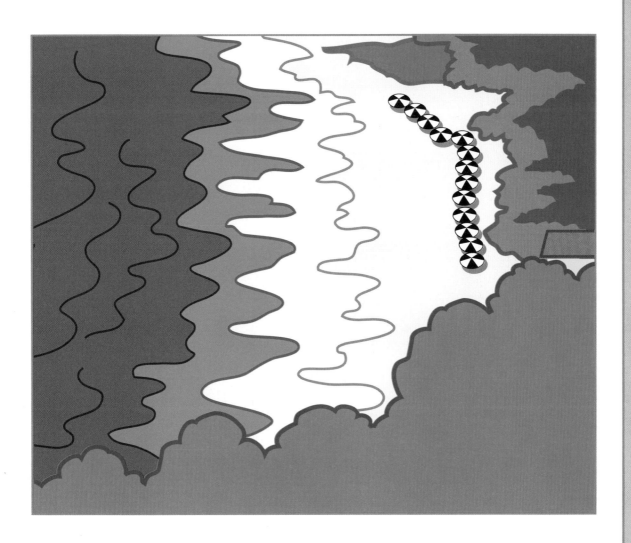

This is a map of that beach. Find the sand, the water, and the trees on this map. What else can you find on this map?

Here is a picture of a garden.

Maps use colors to show things.
This map shows the flowers in the
garden. Can you find the purple
flowers on this map?

This picture shows what a neighborhood looks like from above.

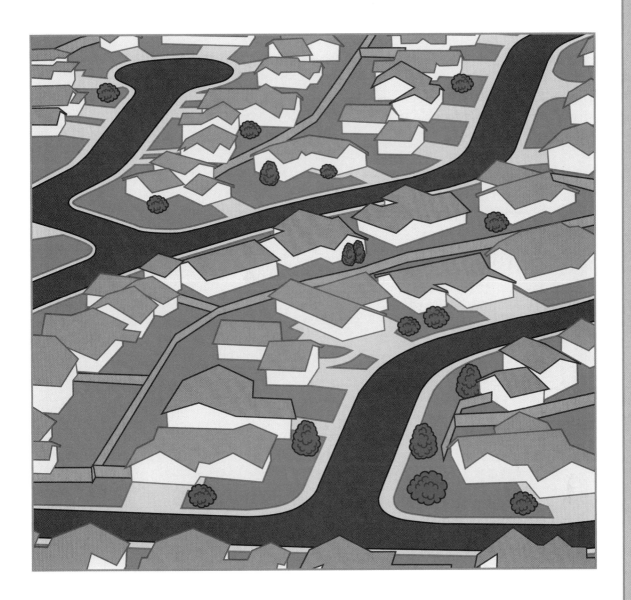

This is a map of that neighborhood. What can you see from above that you cannot see from the ground?

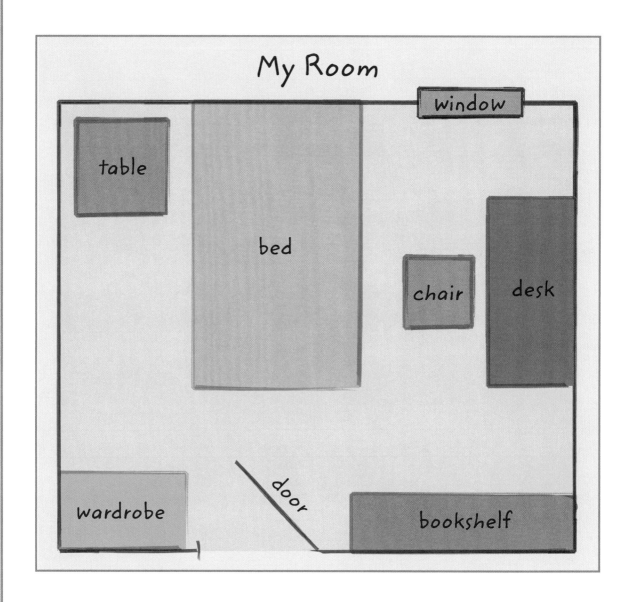

A map can show a small place.
A bedroom is a small place.

My Country

A map can show a big place. This map shows the United States. The United States is much bigger than a bedroom. But the maps are about the same size.

Parts of a Map

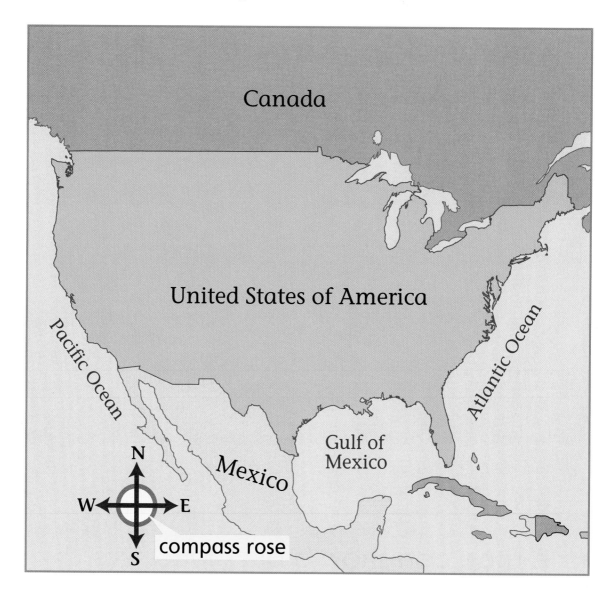

The compass rose on a map helps you read direction. North is at the top of a map. South is at the bottom. East is on the right, and west is on the left.

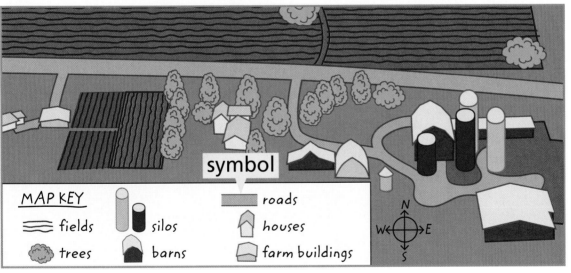

symbol

MAP KEY
≋ fields   silos   roads
🌳 trees   barns   houses
                     farm buildings

N
W—E
S

Symbols are pictures that stand for something. Symbols help you read maps, too. Look at the map key. It shows what the symbols on this map mean.

How Do People Use Maps?

People use maps in many ways. They use maps to help find where things are. They use maps to get from place to place.

People use maps to find places in their state. They also use maps to find places in their country.

What Is a Globe?

A **globe** is a model of the Earth. It is round like a ball. A globe helps you see where everything is in the world.

Think and Respond

Strategy: Ask Questions

Trace your hand.

Write 5 questions about "What Is a Map?"

What Is a Map?

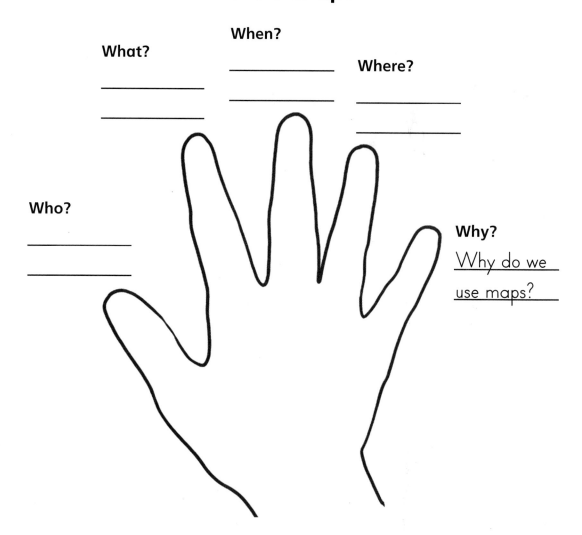

What?
_____
_____

When?
_____

Where?
_____
_____

Who?
_____
_____

Why?
Why do we
use maps?

Interview a Partner

Use the picture of your hand.

Ask a partner your questions about maps.

Talk It Over

1 What will you tell a friend about maps?

2 Name two tools you can use to find new places.

3 Think about the two stories in this unit.

What do these stories say about getting from one place to another?

Content Connections

Play a Directions Game

Where is the bank?

partners

1. Play a game with a map.
2. Ask a friend for directions.
3. Follow the directions with your finger.

Make a Globe

small group

1. Use a balloon and some newspaper.
2. Make a model of the Earth.
3. Paint the oceans and land.
4. Tell about your globe.

Make a Landforms Movie
Internet

small group

1. Find information about landforms.

2. Draw and label landforms for a movie.

3. Talk about the landforms.

mountain

WRITING

Write a Poem

on your own

1. Talk about a place in your neighborhood.

2. Describe things you see, hear, and smell.

3. Write a poem.

At the Bakery

I see tall cakes,

I hear happy music,

I smell fresh bread,

at the bakery!

Words That Tell Where

Listen and sing.

Song

All Over the Map

Down the street,
Across the town,
Over the bridge, all around,
On the map I walk for miles
With my fingers!

Tune: "London Bridge"

Let's Learn!

Some words tell where things are.

across	I go **across** the park.
over	I go **over** the bridge.
down	I go **down** the street.
by	I go **by** the store.

Where is the map?

It is on the wall.

Let's Talk!

Ask a question about where something is. Listen to your partner's answer.

Let's Write!

Write a sentence about where something is.

Draw a picture.

My globe is on my desk.

Show What You Know

Look back at the pictures this unit.

Tell about the places you can see in the pictures.

Places We See

From Here to There	Mama Talks Too Much	What is a Map?
María's house her town the United States the solar system		

Share Your Work

Draw a picture of your neighborhood.

Tell about your favorite places.

Put your picture in a class book.

Read and Learn More

Leveled Books

Far Away
by Salvador Sarmiento

One Afternoon
by Yumi Heo

Theme Library

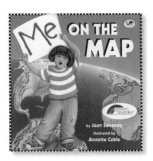

Whoever You Are
by Mem Fox

Me on the Map
by Joan Sweeney

Internet

Go to: www.hbavenues.com

What Do You Do?

Around the Neighborhood

Maps, Maps, Maps

195

A B C D E F G H I J K L M N O P Q R S T U V W X Y Z

A

as

Hana is **as** tall **as** Alex.

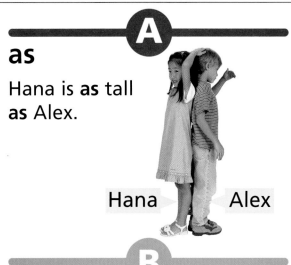

Hana   Alex

B

build

People **build** many things. They use tools.

saw

shovel

hammer

nail

by

We walk **by** the lake.

C

called

Yesterday, Sak **called** his grandmother on the telephone.

telephone

close

Mia and Jody skate **close** to each other.

Mia   Jody

come along

Come along, Fluffy!

each

The teacher gives **each** student a book.

eggs

Some animals hatch from **eggs**.

baby bird   duckling

find

Nadia lost her book. Where did she **find** it?

first

I brush my teeth **first**. Then I comb my hair.

from

We walk **from** the house to the car.

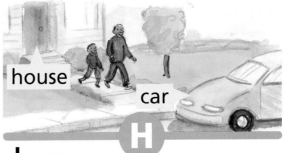

house   car

here

Spot, bring the ball **here**.

ball

house

I live in this **house**.

how

Carlos can jump rope. He knows **how** to do it.

a b c d e f g h i j k l m n o p q r s t u v w x y z

197

A B C D E F G H I J K L M N O P Q R S T U V W X Y Z

L

live

Lisa and Kenny **live** at 28 Clark Road.

M

make

Gil can **make** a sandwich.

sandwich

map

A **map** can help you learn about a place.

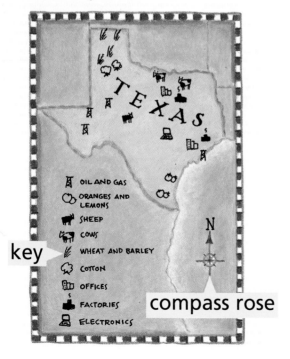

key

compass rose

more

Rob has **more** books than Jana. Lisa has the most books.

Jana

Lisa

Rob

more

the most

N

name

The **name** of this dog is Fluffy.

name

now

It is raining **now**!

our

We love **our** grandmother.

grandmother

P

people

These **people** are camping.

people

person

place

This is a beach. We like this **place**!

beach

S

said

Jan talked to Bill. She **said** many things.

Bill

Jan

say

What did you **say**? I can't hear you.

see

He needs glasses to **see** well.

glasses

shows

He **shows** his new jacket to his sister.

price tag

small

The box is too **small**. The ball will not go in.

big ball

small box

a b c d e f g h i j k l m n o p q r s t u v w x y z

199

A
B
C
D
E
F
G
H
I
J
K
L
M
N
O
P
Q
R
S
T
U
V
W
X
Y
Z

so

Mia is tired, **so** she goes to bed.

something

Something is in the bag. What is it?

stop

The cars **stop** at the red light.

red light

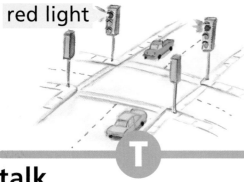

T

talk

We **talk** on the phone every Saturday.

than

I am older **than** I was last year.

last year   now

their

Celia and Josie do **their** homework.

pencil

there

Lin's book is **there**.

they

The boys have fun. **They** ride bikes.

helmet

bike

things

Do you have these **things** at school?

 pencil glue scissors

 eraser ruler crayon

this

This is my cat. That is my dog.

 this

that

too

These clothes are **too** big!

U

use

I **use** crayons to draw a picture.

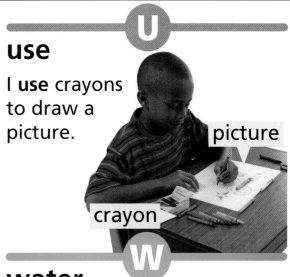

picture

crayon

W

water

You can find **water** in rivers, lakes, and oceans.

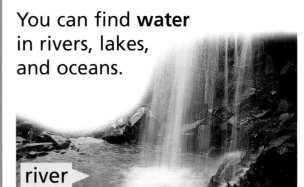

river

way

This is the **way** I make my bed.

bed

were

We **were** at the beach yesterday.

A B C D E F G H I J K L M N O P Q R S T U V W X Y Z

what

What do you like to eat?

egg

peach

carrot

sandwich

when

❶ We play outside **when** it snows.

when

❷ **When** does your school start?

8:00 a.m.

8:30 a.m.

9:00 a.m.

where

Where is the cat?

who

Who has a blue balloon?
Megan has a blue balloon.

Tanya   Hugo   Megan

with

I am in the car **with** Dad.

Acknowledgments continued

Little, Brown and Company: *Come Along, Daisy!* by Jane Simmons. Copyright © 1997 by Jane Simmons. By permission of Little, Brown and Company, (Inc.)

Marian Reiner: "¡Hola, niño!" from *I Never Did That Before* by Lilian Moore. Copyright © 1995 by Lilian Moore. Used by permission of Marian Reiner for the author.

Yellow Umbrella Books: *What Is a Map?* by Lauren Weidenman. © 2001 by Yellow Umbrella Books: Social Studies, an imprint of Capstone Press. Used with permission.

Photographs:

p5 and pp128-129: courtesy of Workman Publishing, New York, from *My World & Globe* by Ira Wolfman, illustrated by Paul Meisel (inflatable globe).

Animals Animals/Earth Scenes: p76 (frog jumping, © Stephen Dalton/OSF), pp86-87 (killdeer, © James Robinson and fawn, © Leonard Rue), p185 (farm, © Ken Cole).

Bruce Coleman, Inc.: p68 and p72 (turtle, © Joe McDonald), p74 (turtles hatching, © E.R. Degginger), p78 (duck, © Donald White), p80 (duck and ducklings, © Scott Nielson), p81 (duck quacking and ducklings, © Scott Nielson), p197 (ducklings hatching, © Scott Nielson).

CORBIS: (all © CORBIS) p8 (farmhouse, © Darrell Gulin and house, © Lester Lefkowitz), p12 and p14 (house in Somalia, © Kevin Fleming) p12 and p15 (house in Nepal, © Enzo and Paolo Ragazzini), p17 (house in Ghana, © Margaret Courtney-Clarke), p18 (house in Mexico, © Kelly-Mooney Photography), p21 (family, © Lindsay Hebberd), p23 (turkey dinner, © Steve Chenn), p76 (frog eggs, © Martin B. Withers/Frank Lane Picture Agency), p80 (ducks, © Gary W. Carter), p180 (neighborhood), p186 (kids and map, © Phil Shermeister).

Digital Studios: p24 (pencil), p201 (glue), p202 (egg).

Digital Vision: p201 (girls playing dress-up).

Getty Images, Inc.: (all © Getty Images) p3 and p13 (hammer and nails, © PhotoDisc), p4 and pp62-63 (butterfly, © Ryan/Beyer/The Image Bank), p12 and p15 (rocks, © PhotoDisc), p16 (men building palm roof, © David Hiser/Stone), p19 (homes in Argentina, © Inner Light/ The Image Bank and paintbrush, © PhotoDisc), p20 (grapes, © Artville and persimmons, © PhotoDisc), p23 (leaves, © PhotoDisc), p24 (mouse, © PhotoDisc), p25 (ribbons, © PhotoDisc), p69 (eggs, © PhotoDisc), p169 (boy recycling, © 203PhotoDisc), p178 (flower garden, © D J Ball/Stone), p200 (paper sack, © PhotoDisc), p201

(pencil, scissors, eraser, ruler, peach and sandwich, © Artville), p202 (family in snow, © PhotoDisc).

ImageState: p176 (beach).

Index Stock Imagery: p8 (adobe house, © Ernesto Burciaga and cabin, © Scott Berner), pp174-175 (kids and map, © Martin Fox), p199 (girl with grandmother, © Benelux Press).

National Geographic Society: p197 (boy on bike, © Joseph H. Bailey).

New Century Graphics: pp12-13 (wood), p16 (bamboo), p22 (mat background), p56 (cardboard house and paper geese), p57 (shoes), pp71-73, 77-79 (spiral notebook), p128-129 (inflatable globes), p129 (card), p201 (crayon), p202 (clocks).

PhotoEdit, Inc.: p13 (building house, © A. Ramey), p24 (doing homework, © Patrick Olear), p25 (birthday party, © Bill Bachman), p130 (supermarket, © Susan Van Etten), p131 (grocery store, © Tony Freeman), p135 (city street, © Rudi Von Briel), p187 and p189 (family with map, © Michael Newman), p196 (ice skating, © Barbara Stitzer), p199 (camping, © Nancy Sheehan).

Photo Researchers, Inc.: p201 (waterfall, © Jim Zipp).

PictureQuest LLC: (all © PictureQuest) p8 (mobile home, © Michael Dwyer/Stock Boston Inc.), p14 (branches, © Ryan McVay/PhotoDisc), p20 (woman, © Bob Daemmrich/Stock Boston Inc.), p21 (petals, © Edward Cross/photo library), p131 (father and daughter shopping, and policeman talking to girls, © Bob Daemmrich/Stock Boston Inc.), p196 (walking by lake, © Andre Henny/Focus Group), p197 (baby birds, © Jeff Foott/ Discovery Images), p199 (family on beach, © Bill Bachman/eStock Photography), p200 (girls doing homework, © David Stover/ Stock South).

Stockbyte: p18 (paint can and brush), p202 (carrot and kids at beach).

Johnny Sundby: p59 (boy), p86 (boy).

The Image Works: p25 (girls in Japan, © The Image Works/Hideo Haga/Haga), p198 (raining, © J. Crawford).

Elizabeth Garza Williams: pp3, 6-7 (father and daughter), p4 and p80 (boy with binoculars), p5, p187 and p194 (boy with globe), p7 (hand), p8 (apartments), p9 (bedroom), p10 (boy with paint), p27 (kids), p28 (girl with art), p30 (boy), p56 (kids drawing), p59 (kids), p63 (hand with butterfly), p69 (boy with egg), p70 (boy looking at eggs), p75 (boy pointing), p83 (kids) p84 (girl with cards and boy jumping), p122 (boy with dragonfly and kids singing),

p125 (kids), pp128-129 (girl with globes), p130 (school), p131 (doctor and patient), p167 (kids), p168 (kids), p169 (girl raising hand), p170 (girl), p190 (kids), p192 (hand), p193 (kids), p196 (girl and boy comparing height), p197 (boy jumping rope), p199 (boy with glasses), p200 (young boy, older boy and girl in library), p201 (boy coloring).

Author and Illustrator Photos:

p55 courtesy of Alexi Natchev, p119 courtesy of Jane Simmons, p163 Marisabina Russo, courtesy of HarperCollins.

Illustrations:

Selina Alko: pp172-173 (Our Map); **Martha Avilés:** pp164-165 (¡Hola, niño!); **Steve Bjorkman:** pp30-31 (The Three Little Pigs), pp66-67 (How Do You Make a Nest?); **Hannah Bonner:** p71, p73, p77, p79 (*Eggs*); **Karen Stormer Brooks:** pp170-171, p195 (A Trip to the Library); **Lynne Cravath:** pp132-133 (Nick's Day); **Diane Greenseid:** pp88-89 (Come Along!); **Theresa Flavin:** p196 (Build) **Peter Grosshauser:** p32-33 (Mouse House); **Grace Lin:** p58 (Cake); **Lori Lohstoeter:** p124 (Five Little Eggs); **Alexi Natchev:** p3, pp34-55, and p60 (*Honza's Little House*); **Marisabina Russo:** p5, pp134-163 (*Mama Talks Too Much*); **Roni Shepherd:** p196 (called, come along), p197 (each, find, first, from, here), p198 (live, more, name, make), p199 (said, say, small, show), p200 (so, stop, they, talk), p201 (this, way, were) p202 (where, with); **Jane Simmons:** p4, pp90-123 and p127 (*Come Along, Daisy!*); **John Roman:** p192 (All Over the Map); **Rosiland Solomon:** pp64-65 (Growing Things), p123 (birds); **Anne Wilson:** pp10-11 (Welcome Home!); **Elizabeth Wolf:** p198 (map).

The Avenues Development Team

Hampton-Brown extends special thanks to the following staff who contributed so much to the creation of the Grade 1 and 2 Pupil Editions.

Editorial: Renee Biermann, Susan Buntrock, Julie Cason, Honor Cline, Shirleyann Costigan, Roseann Erwin, Kristin FitzPatrick, Margot Hanis, Mary Hawley, Fredrick Ignacio, Phillip Kennedy, Dawn Liseth, Sheron Long, and Ann Seivert.

Design and Production: Chaos Factory and Associates, Kim Cockrum, Sherry Corley, Darius Detwiler, Jeri Gibson, Raymond Ortiz Godfrey, Delaina Hodgden, Raymond Hoffmeyer, Rick Holcomb, Leslie McDonald, Michael Moore, Andrea Pastrano-Tamez, Stephanie Rice, Augustine Rivera, Debbie Saxton, Curtis Spitler, Jonni Stains, Alicia Sternberg, Debbie Wright Swisher, Andrea Erin Thompson, Terry Taylor, Teri Wilson, and Hoshin Woo.

Permissions: Barbara Mathewson.

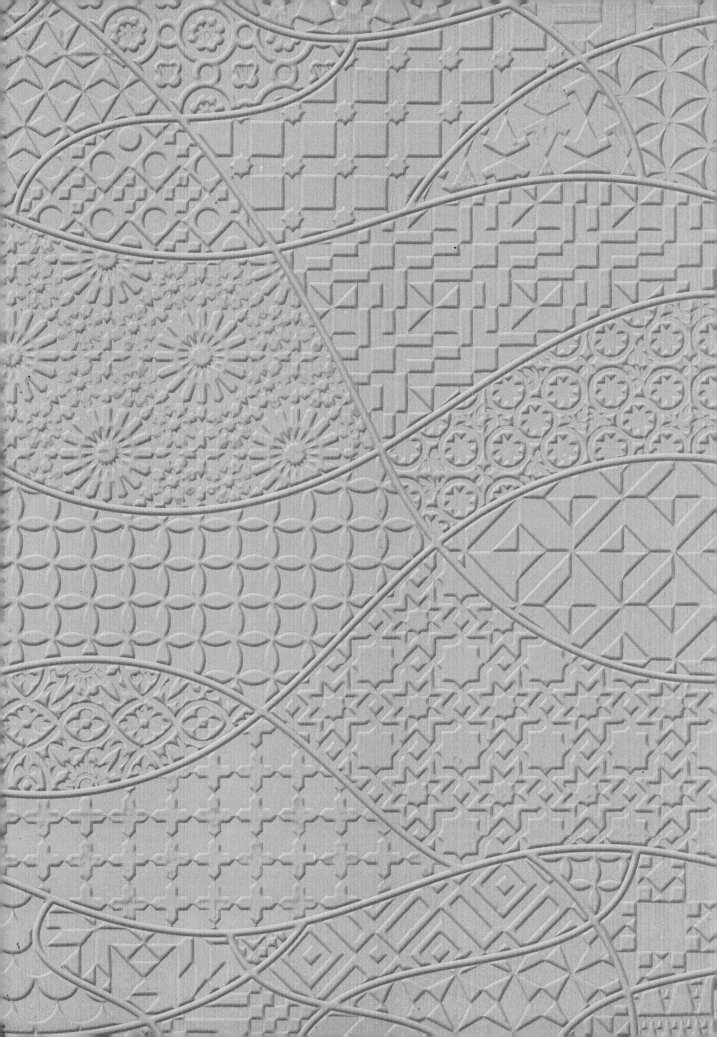